Tell Me a Story

Contents

Features

WORD BUILDER

Have you ever wondered what the difference is between a myth and a legend? Find out on page 5.

TRY THIS!

Read about clay Storyteller figures on page 12. Then follow the steps in **Mould a Story** on page 14 to make your own Storyteller.

IN FOCUS

Read an interview with a larger-than-life storyteller in **Bringing Stories to Life** on page 18.

PROFILE

Do you know who wrote one hundred and fifty-six fairy tales? Learn about this famous author in **A Love of Stories** on page 28.

SITESEEING · ART & ENTERTAINMENT

Where did the story of Cinderella come from?

Visit www.infosteps.co.uk for more about **STORIES**.

Once Upon a Time

Since the beginning of time people have told stories. Long before books were printed or people first learned to read and write they told each other tales, myths, legends and **fables**. Some of these stories were made for children. Others were only for adults.

Stories have many purposes. Some stories are just for fun. Others have a message or teach a lesson. Some stories are from long ago, filled with family history. Others are like dreams of what may happen in the future.

Since early times Native American children have learned their tribal history and customs through the retelling of myths and legends.

WORD BUILDER

A myth is a traditional story that explains how something came to be the way it is. Myths often contain imaginary people or gods and goddesses.

A legend is a traditional story that is sometimes based on a real event or a real person.

5

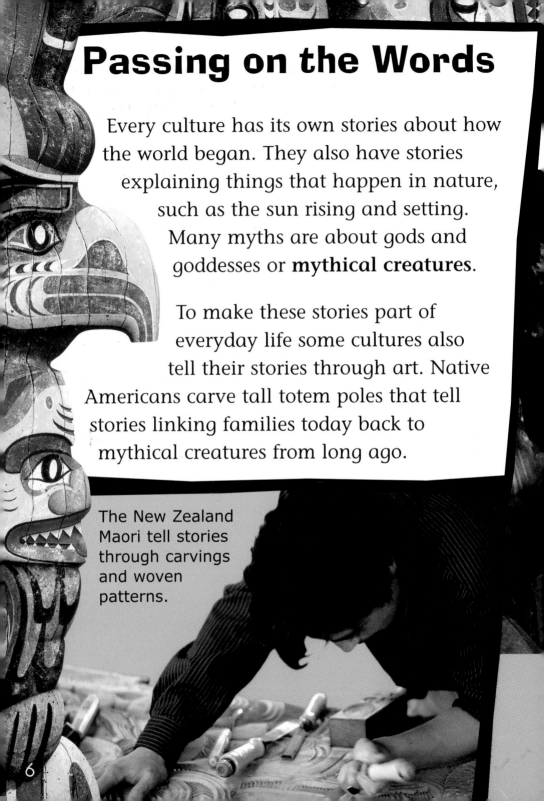

Passing on the Words

Every culture has its own stories about how the world began. They also have stories explaining things that happen in nature, such as the sun rising and setting. Many myths are about gods and goddesses or **mythical creatures**.

To make these stories part of everyday life some cultures also tell their stories through art. Native Americans carve tall totem poles that tell stories linking families today back to mythical creatures from long ago.

The New Zealand Maori tell stories through carvings and woven patterns.

Many cultures use masks to help them tell stories. Masks can be used to show different types of characters. They can also show emotions such as anger and joy.

The Aboriginal people of Australia have many different stories of how the world came to be. These are called stories of the Dreamtime. By telling or acting out stories they keep their culture and history alive.

Like many cultures the ancient Egyptians passed their stories down from parent to child. In this way stories could live on for thousands of years without ever being written.

The ancient Greeks believed that gods and goddesses lived on top of a mountain named Mount Olympus. They told many stories about these gods and goddesses who looked and behaved like humans. The people thought that the gods and goddesses could control nature and future events.

The ancient Chinese told a myth about how the world began. They said it was made by Pan Gu, who formed the sun, moon and stars and floated them in space.

In Greek mythology Zeus was the king of the gods. He roared with thunder and threw lightning bolts when he was angry.

HOMER

Many people believe that a man named Homer was one of the greatest storytellers who ever lived. Not much is known about Homer, except that he was Greek and he lived around 2,800 years ago. It is believed that Homer was blind and could not read or write.

Homer made up two very long, very clever **epics** called the *Iliad* and the *Odyssey*. It is thought that parts of the poems really happened. Other parts were made up. Because these poems were too long to remember word-for-word Homer probably told them a little differently every time. Other storytellers continued to tell Homer's poems after his death. Later they were written down.

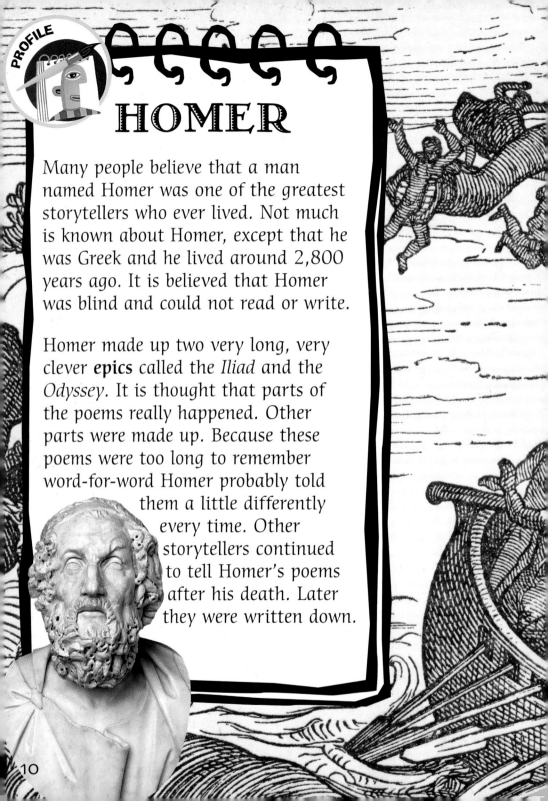

The main character of the *Odyssey* is a man named Odysseus who makes a journey that lasts ten years. On the way he has to sail past the cave of a six-headed monster.

Storyteller Art

For many years some Native Americans have created clay figures of talking people or animals as a reminder of different stories. These figures are called Storytellers. Usually the Storytellers are made with children or baby animals sitting on them, listening to their stories.

Sometimes even the patterns painted on the Storytellers have a story of their own. Artists who make Storytellers pass on their patterns to their children in the same way as stories are passed on.

Storyteller figures are often animals. The animals usually learn a lesson in their story. Then the animal becomes the Storyteller and tells its story to the little ones.

Many Storytellers have drums to help people remember the rhythm of the stories.

13

Mould a Story

Mould your own Storyteller figure to remind yourself of your favourite story. You can use clay or salt dough.

Salt Dough

You will need:
- 2 cups flour
- 1 cup salt
- 1 cup water

1. Mix flour, salt and water.

2. Knead dough into a firm ball.

3. Add more flour or water as needed.

4. Form figure.

5. Dry in a warm place or bake at 180°C for 45-50 minutes.

1 Decide what kind of Storyteller you would like to make. Mould a shape for the body. Add a head.

2 Roll out arms and/or legs (depending on if your Storyteller is a person or an animal). Join them to the body.

3 Mould some little babies.

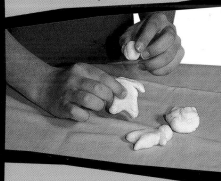

4 When your Storyteller is dry paint it. Remember to add some interesting patterns.

5 Glue the babies onto your Storyteller. Now show your Storyteller to friends and tell them your story.

15

Storytelling Through the Ages

In many cultures the people who pass on stories, legends and tales are very important people. Long ago in northern Europe storytellers were known as skalds. When the king went into battle he would take his skald with him to tell tales of the king's bravery. In Ireland, Scotland and Wales the best storytellers used to be called bards. Young storytellers had to study hard and learn all the important stories before they could become a bard.

Skald

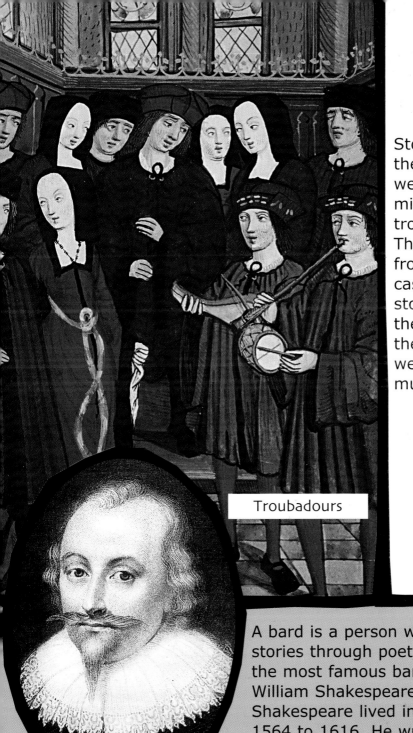

Storytellers in the **Middle Ages** were called minstrels or troubadours. They travelled from castle to castle telling stories wherever they went. Often these stories were told to music.

Troubadours

A bard is a person who tells stories through poetry. Perhaps the most famous bard of all is William Shakespeare, Bard of Avon. Shakespeare lived in England from 1564 to 1616. He wrote at least thirty-seven plays and many poems.

Bard

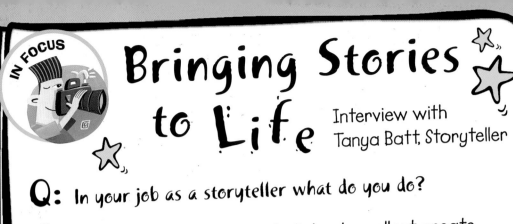

IN FOCUS

Bringing Stories to Life

Interview with
Tanya Batt, Storyteller

Q: In your job as a storyteller what do you do?

A: As a storyteller, my job is to listen to, collect, create and tell stories. I share the stories with people of all ages. I tell stories in schools, early childhood centres, libraries, community centres, theatres, universities, parks, hospitals and museums.
I tell stories because I love them.

Q: Do you make up your own stories or do you use other people's stories?

A: I do both. Some stories I read in books, some I hear from other people and some I make up myself. I like taking well-known tales and retelling them with a new twist.

It is always polite to ask someone if you can tell their story, just like you would ask permission to borrow their clothes or share their food.

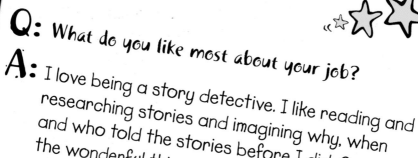

Q: What do you like most about your job?

A: I love being a story detective. I like reading and researching stories and imagining why, when and who told the stories before I did. One of the wonderful things about stories is that you can travel forward and backwards in time and visit magical worlds without having to leave your seat. Using your imagination you can go anywhere.

Q: Why did you become a storyteller?

A: I have the great fortune of belonging to a family where everyone loves stories. When I was a child we lived in the outback of Australia and car journeys were very long and boring. I used to talk and tell stories to pass the time. My mother said I could talk for 900 kilometres without stopping.

Storytelling became a natural channel for my love of words, expressing myself and my strong imagination. I tell stories because they remind me of the mystery and magic of the world we live in.

Q: Your storytelling costumes are fantastic. Do you make them yourself?

A: When I first started telling stories I made my own costumes. These days I am very lucky to have a clever designer and friend who makes my costumes for me. Not all storytellers wear costumes. I do because I love dressing up. I have a mermaid, a fairy, a queen, an Arabian princess and a safari costume, to name a few. When I dress up I feel like I become part of a story.

21

Rhymes for the Nursery

Parents have always told stories, sung songs and whispered **nonsense rhymes** to their children. Some are about real people or real things. Others are made up. Today we call these little stories "nursery rhymes". Before the 1820s they were simply called ditties or "Mother Goose" songs. Nobody knows who Mother Goose was, but her stories have been famous across the Western world for over 200 years.

Little Miss Muffet

Little Miss Muffet was probably a girl named Patience Muffet who was born in the late 1500s. Her father was a famous scientist who studied insects. However, we don't know if Patience was really scared of spiders!

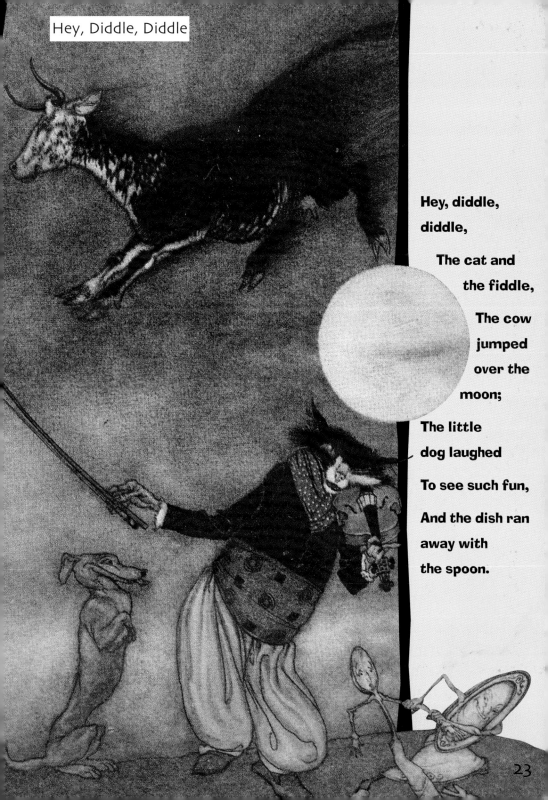

Hey, diddle,
diddle,

The cat and
the fiddle,

The cow
jumped
over the
moon;

The little
dog laughed

To see such fun,

And the dish ran
away with
the spoon.

23

The funny thing is many of these nursery rhymes were not made for children. Adults used rhymes to spread ideas and gossip in a clever way so that no one would get in trouble for speaking against the powerful people of the time.

Some rhymes were short versions of popular adult songs or stories. Others spoke of famous people.

The contrary Mary in this rhyme is thought to have been **Mary, Queen of Scots**. She was not very popular and this rhyme was probably invented to make fun of her.

24

Little Jack Horner

Legend says that in the 1500s a man named Jack Horner was given the job of delivering a special pie to the King of England. Inside the pie were the ownership papers to twelve large houses. On the journey sneaky Jack "put in his thumb and pulled out a plum"—the ownership papers to the grandest house, which he then kept.

25

Fairy-Tale Fun

Fairy tales are **folktales** about ordinary people or animals with a sprinkling of magical make-believe added for fun. Many of these stories begin with "Once upon a time . . . " and often parts of the story are repeated over and over to make them easy to remember.

When it comes to "baddies" fairy tales have quite a few. Giants, goblins, witches and wolves are popular villains. Fairies and elves are often "goodies" who save the day. Thanks to the goodies most fairy tales end with everyone living "happily ever after".

The number three is a popular fairy-tale number.

The fairy tale of Little Red Riding Hood came from France. In the first story Little Red Riding Hood was eaten by the wolf and the story ended there. Later a woodcutter who rescued Red Riding Hood and her grandmother was added to the story.

Where did the story of Cinderella come from?

Visit **www.infosteps.co.uk**
for more about **STORIES.**

A LOVE OF STORIES

Hans Christian Andersen (1805-1875)

Hans Christian Andersen was the author of many of the world's most famous fairy tales. He was born in Denmark in 1805 to a poor family. When he left school Hans hoped to earn a living as an actor, singer and dancer. But it was hard to find work so he started writing instead. At first he wrote books and plays for adults, but soon fairy tales took over. By the time he died in 1875 Hans Christian Andersen had written one hundred and fifty-six fairy tales.

The Princess and the Pea

Take the Challenge!

List all the stories by Hans Christian Andersen that you can think of. Use the library or Internet to help you.

Glossary

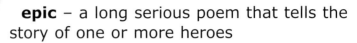

epic – a long serious poem that tells the story of one or more heroes

fable – a very short story that teaches a lesson. Fables are usually about animals that talk.

folktale – a story that has been handed down from generation to generation

Mary, Queen of Scots – the queen of Scotland from 1542 to 1587. Some people think that the "silver bells and cockle shells" talked about in the nursery rhyme were decorations on a dress of hers. The "pretty maids all in a row" were possibly the four women, called ladies-in-waiting, who helped look after the queen.

Middle Ages – the name for a period of time in western Europe between ancient and modern times. The Middle Ages began about the year 600 and ended about the year 1500.

mythical creature – an imaginary creature, often with special powers, from a myth or other story. In a well-known Greek legend the hero Heracles had to kill a mythical snake with 100 heads. Unicorns, dragons and winged horses are also mythical creatures.

nonsense rhyme – a rhyme or poem that is just for fun and does not seem to make sense

Index

Discussion Starters

1 Some cultures use carving or weaving to help them tell their stories. Some make Storyteller figures. Can you think of other ways stories can be told through art? What are they?

2 Some nursery rhymes are about real people or real things. Choose one of your favourite nursery rhymes and make up a story behind the rhyme. Does it sound believable? Why or why not?

3 Most fairy tales have "baddies" and "goodies". Why do you think giants, goblins, witches and wolves are often the bad characters in stories? What would happen if you made these characters good instead?